W9-DIJ-116

Katy Perry

By Robin Johnson

Crabtree Publishing Company

www.crabtreebooks.com

Crabtree Publishing Company

www.crabtreebooks.com

Author: Robin Johnson
Publishing plan research and development:
  Sean Charlebois, Reagan Miller
  Crabtree Publishing Company
Project coordinator: Kathy Middleton
Photo research: Crystal Sikkens
Editor: Molly Aloian
Proofreader: Crystal Sikkens
Designer: Ken Wright
**Production coordinator and Prepress
  technician:** Ken Wright

Photographs:
Associated Press: pages 20, 24, 24
BigStockPhoto: pages 11, 17
Dreamstime: pages 10, 23
Getty Images: Jesse Grant/Stringer: pages
  9 (left), 14; Florian Seefried: page 9 (right)
iStockphoto: page 16
Keystone Press: ZUMApress.com: cover;
  Mavrixphoto.com: pages 6, 18; BEImages:
  page 8; Byron Purvis/AdMedia: page 12;
  COP/BuzzFoto.com: page 15; BIGPictures
  UK: page 22; Photoshot/AdMedia: page 25;
  Isabella Conway/Broadimage: page 26
Shutterstock: pages 1, 4, 5, 7, 21, 27, 28

Every effort has been made to trace copyright holders and to obtain their permission for use of copyright material. The authors and publishers would be pleased to rectify any error or omission in future editions. All the Internet addresses given in this book were correct at the time of going to press. The author and publishers regret any inconvenience caused if addresses have changed or sites have ceased to exist, but can accept no responsibility for any such changes.

Library and Archives Canada Cataloguing in Publication

Johnson, Robin (Robin R.)
    Katy Perry / Robin Johnson.

(Superstars!)
Includes index.
Issued also in an electronic format.
ISBN 978-0-7787-7608-6 (bound).--ISBN 978-0-7787-7613-0 (pbk.)

    1. Perry, Katy--Juvenile literature. 2. Singers--United States--Biography--Juvenile literature. I. Title. II. Series: Superstars! (St. Catharines, Ont.)

ML3930.P463J69 2011   j782.42164092   C2011-905253-9

Library of Congress Cataloging-in-Publication Data

Johnson, Robin (Robin R.)
    Katy Perry / by Robin Johnson.
        p. cm. -- (Superstars!)
    Includes index.
    ISBN 978-0-7787-7608-6 (reinforced library binding : alk. paper) --
ISBN 978-0-7787-7613-0 (pbk. : alk. paper) -- ISBN 978-1-4271-8854-8
(electronic pdf) -- ISBN 978-1-4271-9757-3 (electronic html)
    1. Perry, Katy--Juvenile literature. 2. Singers--United States--Biography--Juvenile literature. I. Title. II. Series.

    ML3930.P455J64 2012
    782.42164092--dc23
    [B]
                                                                                              2011029843

Crabtree Publishing Company

www.crabtreebooks.com   1-800-387-7650

Printed in Canada/082011/MA20110714

Published in Canada
Crabtree Publishing
616 Welland Ave.
St. Catharines, ON
L2M 5V6

Published in the United States
Crabtree Publishing
PMB 59051
350 Fifth Avenue, 59th Floor
New York, New York 10118

Published in the United Kingdom
Crabtree Publishing
Maritime House
Basin Road North, Hove
BN41 1WR

Published in Australia
Crabtree Publishing
3 Charles Street
Coburg North
VIC 3058

CONTENTS

Words that are defined in the glossary are in **bold** type the first time they appear in the text.

Hello Katy!

Katy Perry is the **quirky** pop superstar who has attracted millions of adoring young fans. Katy's catchy tune "I Kissed a Girl" got toes tapping and fingers snapping around the world. It also made Katy an instant international sensation.

Kiss Me, Katy

Katy released the single "I Kissed a Girl" in the spring of 2008. The song captured the attention of music lovers everywhere. Since then, Katy has released two wildly successful studio albums, *One of the Boys* and *Teenage Dream*. She has several hit singles, including "Hot n Cold," "California Gurls," and "Firework." Katy has also **headlined** two worldwide concert tours, entertaining sold-out crowds with her playful music and energetic stage performances.

Gospel Girl

Katy is not a typical pop princess, however. She grew up in a strict Christian home and listened only to **gospel** music. Her first stage was her parents' church and the first album she released was religious rock. Katy learned how to sing, dance, and play guitar at an early age. As she got older, she also learned how to express herself through her music and style.

KATYCATS

Katy Perry is especially popular with preteen and teen girls. Her biggest fans are called "Katycats." Katycats are sassy superfans who love the singer and everything she does. They act like her, dress like her— and think she's absolutely purr-fect!

Katy wows a crowd of snap-happy Katycats during a 2010 performance on the *Today* show.

Very Perry

Today, Katy's songs show the world just who she is. She writes all her own music and **lyrics**. Her songs are based on friendships, romances, breakups, adventures, and other real things that have happened in her life. On her website, KatyPerry.com, the singer says, "If you ever want an answer about how I felt about something or what I was going through or what I believe or my **convictions** or my love, you just have to listen to the lyrics."

Glamour Ninja

Katy also expresses herself through her appearance. The star is known for her fun and fearless fashions. She calls herself a "glamour ninja." Katy often dresses in humorous, colorful outfits that are both glamorous and ridiculous. She enjoys wearing **vintage** clothing she finds at garage sales and thrift stores. She also loves to wear fruit-shaped accessories, especially watermelon.

Katy sweet-talks her fans in a charming cupcake dress.

She Said It

"I love details. I love different colors. I love funny things. I have this one shirt that's got smiley faces as shoulders—so it's really cute and quite humorous. I love a good sense of humor in clothes."
—In an interview in *Seventeen* magazine, February 2009

Cover Girl

Katy is also known for her striking good looks and poster-girl image. The five-foot-eight-inch (1.7-meter) beauty has appeared on the cover of more than 15 magazines. Her long black hair, big blue-green eyes, and natural curves make Katy a picture-perfect choice for any photo shoot.

She Said It

"I called the album Teenage Dream *because I feel like I will always want to be that pin-up poster. I definitely want to be in everybody's dreams at all times..."*
−In an interview in *Women's Health*, April 2009

California Gurl

Katheryn Elizabeth Hudson was born on October 25, 1984. She grew up in Santa Barbara, California. There, she went surfing, skateboarding, and camping. Katy was not a typical California girl, though.

Katy shines with her parents, Mary and Keith Hudson, at a film premiere.

She Said It

"My parents were strict, but it was the world I lived in. I had no idea there was a world outside."
−In an interview in *Women's Health*, April 2009

House Rules

Katy's parents, Keith and Mary, were both **pastors**. They were very strict and religious. Katy was not even allowed to say "deviled eggs"! Her family called them "angeled eggs" instead. Her mother read only the Bible to Katy. Katy was not allowed to read magazines, watch television or movies, or date boys. She was not allowed to listen to secular, or non-religious music. Only gospel music was allowed in her home.

(below) Katy clowns around with her brother David at a record release party for *One of the Boys*.

(above) Katy and her sister Angela strike a pretty pose at a dance party.

Katy in the Middle

Katy grew up with an older sister named Angela and a younger brother named David. They attended Christian school and camps together. As the middle child in her family, Katy always fought for her parents' attention. She sang and performed for them so they would notice her. Katy explains in an interview in *The Times*, "I was just getting whatever attention was left over, and I loved people's reactions, the looks on their faces."

Song and Dance

When she was nine years old, Katy began singing in her parents' church. She also started taking vocal lessons and performing at a local farmers' market twice a week. When she was 13 years old, Katy began playing the guitar. Young Katy also took dance lessons for three years at a local recreation hall. She learned to do the swing and other forties-style dances.

Today, Katy plays both electric and acoustic guitars.

Unique and Different

Katy began forming her sense of style during her early dancing days. She was impressed by the pencil skirts, tight cardigan sweaters, and other vintage clothing the dancers wore. She described their outfits as "unique and different than what was going on in the 2000s." The vintage look would become a big part of Katy's own "unique and different" style.

She Said It

"I started going to Nashville to record some gospel songs, and to be around amazing country-music vets and learn how to craft a song and play guitar. I'd actually have to Superglue the tips of my fingers because they hurt so much from playing guitar all day... And from that, I made the best record I could make as a gospel singer at 15."
–In an interview on MTV.com, June 2008

Katy is Discovered

Katy was discovered when she was 15 years old. She was singing in her parents' church at the time. She began taking trips with her mother to Nashville, Tennessee, to write and record music. Soon, Katy was **signed** by Red Hill, a Christian music **label**. She released her debut, or first, studio album in 2001. *Katy Hudson* was a Christian gospel-rock album. It included the songs "Trust in Me" and "Faith Won't Fail." The album sold only 200 copies because Red Hill Records went out of business that year.

Rebel rocker Alanis Morissette was one of Katy's biggest influences.

Katy Rocks!

As a teenager, Katy began learning about other types of music. Her friends would sneak CDs to her. She would also watch music videos and listen to rock music at their homes. Katy was **influenced** by some of the legendary performers she heard. Katy's biggest influences were British rocker Freddie Mercury and Canadian singer Alanis Morissette. She was also influenced by edgy pop stars Cyndi Lauper, Gwen Stefani, Pat Benatar, Joan Jett, and Garbage's Shirley Manson. These singers all affected how Katy later wrote and performed her music.

Determined to Make It

During her first year of high school, Katy earned her **GED**. Then she left Santa Barbara and moved to Los Angeles. She was 17 years old and determined to make it in the music business. She began working with Glen Ballard, a well-known songwriter and record producer. Katy changed her sound and her style and was ready to change the music world, too.

Looking for Labels

A record label called Island Records signed Katy. She recorded an album but was later dropped from the label. Her album was never released. Katy was then signed by Columbia Records in 2004. She worked with a pop music production team called The Matrix and recorded more songs. Although Katy was named "The Next Big Thing" by *Blender* magazine, Columbia decided to drop her, too.

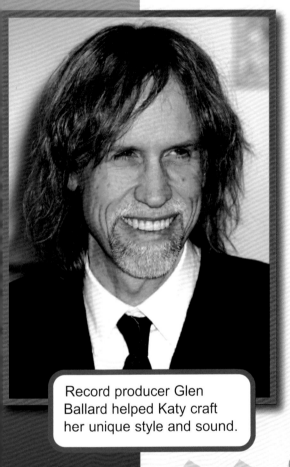

Record producer Glen Ballard helped Katy craft her unique style and sound.

He Said It

"When Katy's father brought her to my studio, I thought she was just going to hand me some music to hear. But she came in with her guitar, and sat right down to play me a song. At that moment, I thought she was extraordinary. She's never had any fear."
−Music producer Glen Ballard in *Rolling Stone* magazine, August 2010

Starving Artist

After three failed recording deals, Katy was almost ready to give up. She was discouraged and defeated, with no money to pay her bills. Katy had given herself a deadline to succeed in the music business, and she was running out of time. In an interview in *Cosmopolitan*, Katy says, "I gave myself until I turned 25 to make it. And if it didn't happen, I thought I'd just try to find a nice husband." Luckily for music lovers everywhere, it did happen for Katy. In 2007, Capitol Records signed the talented 23-year-old performer. (Later, Katy found a nice husband, too!)

WHAT'S IN A NAME?

Katy changed her last name to "Perry." Perry is her mother's maiden name, or the name she had before she was married. Katy changed her name to avoid confusion with a popular American actress named Kate Hudson.

Debut Single

Katy released her debut single on the Internet in November. The song, "Ur So Gay," brought a lot of attention to the young singer. Some praised Katy, calling the song funny and original. Pop megastar Madonna said it was "her favorite song right now." Others did not approve of the song's **controversial** lyrics. Although sales for the single were low, the song got Katy noticed. It also showed the world that Katy Perry was singing a very different tune than other young pop stars.

Sealed with a Kiss

In 2008, Katy Perry rocketed to the top of the charts and became an international singing sensation. Her debut pop album, *One of the Boys*, showed the world that Katy was definitely not one of the boys. It also gave the performer and her adoring fans something to sing about.

Girl Power

Katy released her second single in the spring of 2008. "I Kissed a Girl" was a **breakthrough** hit for Katy. The catchy song topped the Billboard Hot 100 chart in the United States for seven weeks in a row! It also topped the charts in Canada, Australia, the United Kingdom, and many other countries. "I Kissed a Girl" made Katy an international superstar—and sealed her pop future with a kiss.

Katy is pretty in pink and proud of her first hit single.

She Said It

"The media loves to paint this stereotype of good girl gone bad, but that's not how it is. I was raised a bit strict, so I started breaking the rules. I just wanted to carve my own path."

−In an interview in *USA Today*, June 2011

Hit or Miss

Many people think the song "I Kissed a Girl" is playful and fun. It is popular with preteens and teens around the world. In some places, however, the song is banned, or not allowed. Some people do not approve of the song's controversial lyrics and message. They think the song should be kissed goodbye!

Katy and crew shoot the video for her hit single "Hot n Cold." In the video, the singer plays a hot bride whose groom gets cold feet.

One of the Boys

Katy released her first pop album in June 2008. *One of the Boys* featured the hit singles "I Kissed a Girl," "Hot n Cold," "Thinking of You," and "Waking Up in Vegas." The popular songs proved that Katy was not just a one-hit wonder. The album went platinum, which means it sold a million copies. In fact, *One of the Boys* has sold more than five million copies worldwide!

Too Hot to Handle

One of the most popular songs on *One of the Boys* was the single "Hot n Cold." Even Elmo liked it! Katy recorded a new version of the song with the furry red monster for *Sesame Street*. Some parents did not approve of the video, however. They felt that Katy's dress was not suitable for the show's preschool viewers. *Sesame Street* decided to cut the duet from the show. Fans could still watch the video online, however.

SESAME SPLIT

Katy tried to make the best of a bad situation when she found out her video was pulled from *Sesame Street*. She joked about the cancellation on Twitter and poked fun at it during a skit on *Saturday Night Live*.

Katy recorded a kid-friendly version of the song "Hot n Cold" with Elmo. Some parents felt that her dress was not kid-friendly, however.

She Said It

"The stars are aligning for Katy Perry in 2008. I've been working on my record since I was eighteen years old. I've gone through two record labels and written between sixty-five and seventy songs, and now it's ready to come out. It's been a long trip... but the record's here and it's the right one."
—In an interview in Prefixmag.com, February 2008

Warp Speed Ahead

Fans could also watch Katy perform on stage. She went on tour for the first time in the summer of 2008, taking the Vans Warped Tour by storm. The tour is a punk music and extreme sports festival held across the United States and Canada. It features hundreds of bands that play short sets in parking lots and fields. Katy played nearly 50 dates on the tour and wowed even the toughest rockers with her lively performances.

Katy channels her inner punk princess as she performs on the 2008 Vans Warped Tour.

She Kissed a Boy

When Katy was not performing "I Kissed a Girl" on tour, she was kissing her boyfriend! She dated American rapper Travis "Travie" McCoy. Travis is the lead singer of the hip-hop band Gym Class Heroes. The pair dated on and off for several years and spent the summer together on the Vans Warped Tour. Travis even gave Katy a diamond **promise ring**. It didn't work out for the busy couple, though, and they broke up in 2009.

Hello Katy Tour

Katy continued to **promote** her *One of the Boys* album, kicking off her first headlining tour in 2009. The Hello Katy Tour lasted for nearly a year and took the singer to 20 countries in North America, Europe, Asia, and Australia. The concert featured giant blow-up strawberries and other fruit, a huge cat head with glowing eyes, and crazy cat-suit costumes. It also had plenty of on-stage chatter and spunky performances by its headlining superstar.

The 2009 Hello Katy Tour shows the world that Katy Perry is one cool cat.

Teenage Dream

Katy released her third studio album in August 2010. *Teenage Dream* debuted in first place on the Billboard 200. It included the hit singles "California Gurls," "Teenage Dream," "Firework," and "E.T." All four songs reached the top of the Billboard Hot 100—and stayed there for some time. In fact, Katy is the only singer to have had songs in the top ten every week for an entire year! Go Katy!

UNPLUGGED

Katy performed some of her hit songs on *MTV Unplugged*. The songs were made into a live album that was released in November 2009. The album showed the world that the pop sensation is electric even when she is **unplugged!**

Meet Kathy Beth Terry

Katy released *Teenage Dream*'s fifth single, "Last Friday Night (T.G.I.F.)," in June 2011. She introduced her alter ego to the world at the same time. An alter ego is a second personality or a character someone plays. Katy plays the part of Kathy Beth Terry in the song's eight-minute video. Kathy Beth Terry is a nerdy eighth-grade girl with braces and huge glasses. In the eighties-style video for "Last Friday Night (T.G.I.F.)," she wakes up the morning after a big party. A series of clips reveal Kathy Beth Terry gone wild!

She Said It

"My career is like an artichoke. People might think that the leaves are tasty and buttered up and delicious, and they don't even know that there's something magical hidden at the base of it. There's a whole other side [of me] that people didn't know existed."
—In an interview in *Vanity Fair*, May 2011

Rocking the Small Screen

When she is not recording songs, shooting videos, or performing on stage, Katy rocks the small screen! She has entertained viewers on many television talk shows and specials. She was a guest star on the sitcom *How I Met Your Mother*. Katy played herself on the teen drama *Wildfire*, the daytime soap opera *The Young and the Restless*, and the cartoon *The Simpsons*. She was also a guest judge on the talent shows *American Idol* and *The X Factor* and a musical guest on the late-night comedy show *Saturday Night Live*.

Katy pokes fun at her controversial *Sesame Street* video during a comedy skit on *Saturday Night Live*.

She Said It

"I think that people now see that I'm more than just a one-trick-pony...I have a lot more to bring to the table. I'm trying to give people music that they can hopefully adopt as a soundtrack to their lives—songs that speak to a whole range of emotions."
–In an interview in *Elle* magazine, March 2011

Singing Her Praises

Katy also performed and presented awards at the Grammys. Although she has not won a Grammy Award herself, she has been nominated an impressive six times! She was nominated for Album of the Year and Best Pop Vocal Album (for *Teenage Dream*), Best Pop **Collaboration** With Vocals (for "California Gurls" with Snoop Dogg), and Best Female Pop Vocal Performance (three years in a row). The pop superstar has won three People's Choice Awards, two Teen Choice Awards, a Juno Award, and many other prizes. Katy has won awards for her songs, albums, and videos. She even won an award for the best cell phone ringtone!

Katy rocks the red carpet at the 52nd Grammy Awards in 2010.

21

Purr-fectly Perry

Today, Katy continues to thrill audiences with her quirky style and sound. Her latest concert tour proves that she is not just another pretty face in a cupcake hat. She is a larger-than-life entertainer with incredible talent and staying power. There is much more to Katy Perry than just pop music, however. These days, she is feeling Purr-fect and Smurfy—and is happily married!

Sweet as Candy

Katy launched her second concert tour in February 2011. The nine-month California Dreams Tour is a candy-filled extravaganza. The concert tells the story of a girl—named Katy, of course—who lives in a dull, colorless world. She falls asleep and enters a fairy-tale land filled with giant gumdrops and lollipops, candy-cane stairs, and fluffy pink cotton-candy clouds. There's plenty of delicious music in Katy's California Dreams Tour, too. The sweet sounds of the singer fill the air in arenas around the world.

The 2011 California Dreams Tour takes Katy and her candy-coated show to London, England.

Her Favorite Brand

Although she has a very busy tour schedule, Katy always makes time for love. She planned the dates on the California Dreams Tour so she would get one day off with her husband, British comedian Russell Brand, for every two nights she performed. Katy met Russell in the summer of 2008. The two filmed a short scene together for Russell's movie *Get Him to the Greek*. The scene was cut from the film, but it led to romance between the two stars. They began dating the following year. In October 2010, Katy and Russell were married in a small ceremony in India.

Katy and Russell Brand shine at the Los Angeles premiere of *Get Him to the Greek*.

Home Sweet Home

Katy and her husband are both splashy entertainers, but she says their home life is "surprisingly normal." She tries to prepare meals for Russell, but she admits that she is not a very good cook. Katy hopes to start a family with Russell someday, and she thinks he will make a perfect father. In an interview in *Harper's Bazaar*, she says, "I always knew I wanted a great man of God, someone who was going to be an inspiration for people and also be a lovely husband and father...I have all that in him."

Tattoos for Two

Katy and Russell have matching tattoos! They both have the words "Anuugacchati Pravaha" tattooed on their inner right arms. The words are written in Sanskrit, an ancient Indian language, and mean "go with the flow." Katy also has the name "Jesus" tattooed on her left wrist and a smiling strawberry on the inside of her left ankle.

Katy Cares

Katy cares about other people, too, and uses her fame to help them. She supports a number of charities, including the Red Cross, Children's Health Fund, Stand Up to Cancer, and the Humane Society. She performs at fundraisers and benefit concerts around the world. On tour, Katy raises money for charity by selling special light wands that fans can wave during her song "Firework." She would even like to start her own charity with her husband!

Katy performs at the 2009 Life Ball in Vienna, Austria. The annual charity event raises money for people living with HIV and **AIDS**.

In an interview in Britain's *Grazia* magazine, Katy says, "We have this plan to set up a foundation to help people, feed them, clothe them, give shelter. We don't want to use our fame just to sit on our money on a mountain, we want to do something with it."

Hello Kitties!

Katy is crazy about cats! Katy and Russell have three cats—Kitty Purry, Morrissey, and Krusty. She describes Kitty Purry as "the diva of the house." The fluffy gray tabby is a superstar cat! She appeared in Katy's "I Kissed a Girl" video. She was even nominated for the 2009 Teen Choice Award for favorite Celebrity Pet! Sadly, Kitty Purry lost the award to President Obama's dog, Bo.

Katy (center) poses proudly with her perfume at an in-store fragrance signing in Australia.

Sweet Smell of Success

Cat-loving Katy recently introduced a sweet new fragrance to the world. The fruity, vanilla-based perfume is called "Purr." It comes in a pretty purple cat-shaped bottle with jeweled eyes. The scent captures the fun and friskiness of the singer. Katy describes it as "a gorgeous blend of all my favorite scents" and "an absolutely purrfect perfume." Katy is very proud of her perfume and says that she "would stand in front of a train for that little thing."

Smurfs and Muppets

Katy's love of performing brought her to the big screen in 2011. She voices the character Smurfette in the 3-D family film *The Smurfs*. The film's director, Raja Gosnell, chose Katy for the part because she is the perfect mix of sassy and sweet, "giggly and girlish, but sophisticated at the same time." Katy will also make a brief **cameo** appearance in *The Muppets* movie, which hits theaters in November.

A blonde Katy strikes a pose at the New York premiere of *The Smurfs*.

She Said It

"I feel like a walking cartoon most of the time, anyway. It was easy. I got to help shape who [Smurfette] is and give her a twist and more character. I want to do more animation. I think it's such a wonderful teaching tool that brings parents and kids together. I cry in those movies all the time. It's my go-to for a feel-good time."
—In an interview in *USA Today*, June 2011

On Track

Whether Katy continues to create playful pop songs or changes the direction of her career, she is sure to surprise and delight audiences everywhere. In an interview in *Harper's Bazaar*, the superstar singer says, "I am the chief of my train. If [people] want to hop on board, fantastic. There's plenty of room. The KP train is fun." These days, the KP train is definitely on track and moving full steam ahead.

FASHION FORWARD

Katy has said she may also introduce her own fashion line in the future. After all, her outrageous outfits have captured attention on red carpets and stages around the world. The busy singer is in no hurry to take on another new project just yet, however.

Das Auto.

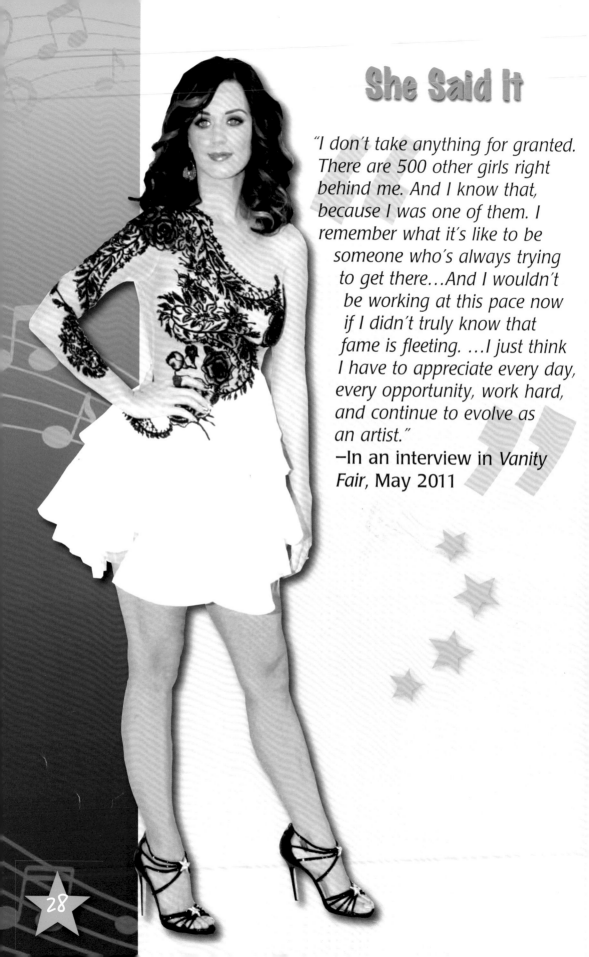

She Said It

"I don't take anything for granted. There are 500 other girls right behind me. And I know that, because I was one of them. I remember what it's like to be someone who's always trying to get there…And I wouldn't be working at this pace now if I didn't truly know that fame is fleeting. …I just think I have to appreciate every day, every opportunity, work hard, and continue to evolve as an artist."
—In an interview in *Vanity Fair*, May 2011

Timeline

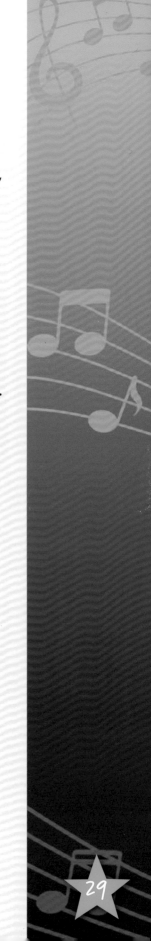

1984: Katheryn Elizabeth Hudson is born in Santa Barbara, California, on October 25.

1999: Fifteen-year-old Katy is discovered while singing in church.

1999: The Christian label Red Hill Records signs Katy, but goes out of business that same year.

2001: Katy's debut studio album, the gospel-rock *Katy Hudson*, is released.

2001: Katy moves to Los Angeles and begins working with record producer Glen Ballard.

2003: Island Records signs Katy, but drops her before her album is released.

2004: Columbia Records signs Katy. She records more songs but is later dropped from that label, too.

2007: Capitol Records signs Katy. She changes her last name from "Hudson" to "Perry."

2007: Katy's first single, "Ur So Gay," is released on the Internet.

2008: Katy's second single, "I Kissed a Girl," is released and rockets the singer to fame.

2008: Katy releases her first pop studio album, *One of the Boys*.

2008: Katy goes punk, playing 50 dates with the summer Vans Warped Tour.

2009: Katy kicks off her first headlining tour, the Hello Katy Tour.

2009: Katy performs some of her hit songs on *MTV Unplugged*, which is made into a live album.

2010: Katy releases her third studio album, *Teenage Dream*.

2010: Katy marries British comedian Russell Brand.

2010: Katy introduces her fragrance, Purr.

2011: Katy launches her California Dreams Tour.

2011: Katy voices the character of Smurfette in *The Smurfs* movie.

Glossary

AIDS A serious disease of the immune system (Acquired Immune Deficiency Syndrome

breakthrough Describing a moment when someone achieves success

cameo A brief appearance by a famous person in a movie, play, or other show

collaboration Working together on a project

controversial Describing something that causes public conflict or disagreement

conviction A belief or opinion that is firmly held

GED A certificate, called General Educational Development, that shows a person has passed tests to complete high school

gospel An emotional style of religious or spiritual singing

headline When a performer is the main attraction in a concert or show

influence To affect or shape someone's life in an important way

label A company that makes and sells recorded music

lyrics The words of a song

pastor The leader of a Christian church

promise ring A ring that means a person would like to marry you someday

promote To share information about a product to help sell it

quirky Having unexpected or unusual traits

sign To be hired by a record company

unplugged Describing music performed without electric instruments

vintage Describing high-quality clothing or other items from the past

Find Out More

Books

Adams, Michelle. *Blue Banner Biography: Katy Perry*. Mitchell Lane Publishers Inc., 2011.

Brown, Anne K. *Katy Perry*. Lucent Books, 2011.

Tieck, Sarah. *Katy Perry: Singing Sensation*. Big Buddy Books, 2011.

Websites

The official Katy Perry website features her music, videos, news, photos, a tour diary, concert updates, and more!
www.katyperry.com

This Katy Perry fan forum has lots of fan-tastic posts and discussions by true Katycats.
http://katyperryforum.com/

Katy Perry's MySpace page includes her blog, photos, links, and about a million of her closest "friends."
www.myspace.com/katyperry

Index

About the Author

Robin Johnson is a freelance author and editor. She has written more than twenty nonfiction children's books, including *The Jonas Brothers*, *Kristen Stewart*, and *Robert Pattinson*. When she isn't working, she divides her time between renovating her home with her husband, taking her two sons to hockey practice, and exploring back roads.